GREEK SACRED SITES

DELPHI
ORACLE OF APOLLO

JILL DUDLEY

PUT IT IN YOUR POCKET SERIES
ORPINGTON PUBLISHERS

Published by
Orpington Publishers

Cover design and origination by
Creeds, Bridport, Dorset
01308 423411

Printed and bound in the UK by
Creeds

© Jill Dudley 2016

ISBN: 978-0-9935378-3-7

DELPHI
ORACLE OF APOLLO

Delphi is situated in one of the most dramatic landscapes having a backdrop of mountains and ravines, and way below it the dry river bed of the Pleistos river filled with silver-grey olive trees. In the far distance the gleaming stretch of the Gulf of Corinth can be glimpsed.

According to Homer's *Hymn to Apollo*, this sacred sanctuary of Apollo was claimed by him in the following manner: one day some merchants (some say they were pirates) were on their way to Pylos from Crete* in a black-prowed galley when Apollo, disguised as a dolphin, leapt out of the sea and landed on the deck. This was regarded as 'a portent great and terrible'. Apollo used his immortal powers to guide the galley towards the coast close to where his new intended sacred site was: *...Then from the ship leaped the Prince, far-darting Apollo, like a star at high noon, while the gledes of fire flew from him, and the splendour flashed to the heavens. Into his inmost Holy Place he went...and in the midst he kindled a flame...* Those who witnessed it were amazed and fearful. Apollo then told the merchants/pirates that they were destined to become his priests.

Apollo was the son of Zeus, supreme god of the ancient world, and the Titaness Leto. Hera, the wife of Zeus, was wildly jealous of these extra-marital affairs of her husband. She had been irate with anger when he had given birth to Athena alone and without her involvement – Athena had been born from his head – and there is a story that the jealous Hera prayed to Gaea (mother earth) that she too might have a child alone and without aid from Zeus. In due course her wish was granted and she immaculately conceived and gave birth to Typhaon, a monstrous creature whom she entrusted to the Dragoness at Delphi. Over the course of time Typhaon and the Dragoness became fused in people's minds and became the Python.

The first thing that Apollo did when he came to Delphi was to slay the Dragoness-Typhaon-Python. Homer describes its death: *...writhing in strong anguish, and mightily panting she lay, rolling about the land. Dread and dire was the din, as she writhed hither and thither through the wood, and gave up the ghost...*

After killing the Python, Apollo took himself north to the Vale of Tempe where he purified himself in the river Peneus. For eight years he served as shepherd to King Admetus of Pherai, in order to atone for the killing of the Python.

Today there is a Sacred Fountain at the centre of a sanctuary of Gaea, the waters of which were said to be guarded by the Python/Dragoness. There is also a story that Gaea had a daughter, a beautiful nymph called Daphne, for whom Apollo developed a passion but, in order to protect her from Apollo's advances, Gaea turned her into a laurel which from then on became sacred to Apollo. It is why winners at the Pythian Games, which commemorated Apollo's eight years of atonement in the Vale of Tempe, were crowned with laurel wreaths.

Those coming to the site overland or by sea would first arrive at the temple of Athena Pronaos on a lower terrace below the main Athens to Delphi road. Pronaos means 'before the temple' and, in her role as protectress of cities, it was fitting for the goddess to have her temple there. Pilgrims would then move on to purify themselves at the Castalian spring at the base of the towering Phaedriades rocks close to the main sanctuary site. The Phaedriades are twin crags from which water issues down a narrow gash. The water cascades into a paved area where the ritual purification took place.

Coming to consult the oracle was a formal process conducted with dignity and ceremony. Having purified himself, the pilgrim would follow the Sacred Way which was at that time flanked by monuments and statues, gifts from city states in gratitude to the oracle's response and advice, each city vying with the other to impress. There were also Treasury Houses, the most notable being the Treasury of the Athenians built in Parian marble which still stands, resembling a miniature temple. The many dedications and votive offerings to Apollo from the Athenian citizens would have been kept inside it.

The temple of Apollo with its numerous tall columns must once have been magnificent on its higher terrace. A pilgrim consulting the oracle would bring what was known as a *pelanos* (an expensive sweetmeat), and a sacrificial animal, usually a goat, which was sprinkled with cold water; if the goat began to tremble, then the enquiry could proceed, if it did not that was the end of it for that day. The custom of using a goat was because it was believed that the sacred source of oracular inspiration was from a cavity in the ground which was first discovered by a goat.

If the signs were auspicious then the goat was sacrificed, and the enquirer, accompanied by the priests, would enter an inner chamber next to the *Adyton,* the most sacred area; there the question would be put to the Pythia (Apollo's priestess) who was seated on her tripod over the cleft in the ground. While seated in this manner, the Pythia held a branch of laurel, and chewed laurel leaves. It is believed she inhaled vapours rising from the cavity which would cause her to fall into a trance. Her responses to the questions put to her often came in the form of riddles which the priests had to interpret.

The temple was aligned to the east so that Apollo's cult statue would have looked out towards the rising sun. His statue was in its most sacred area, the *Adyton,* together with the *Omphalos*. The *Omphalos* was a shoulder-high oval stone believed to have fallen from heaven. Legend has it that Zeus let off two eagles from the far points of the heavens in order to determine the centre of the world; the eagles met at Delphi, thus settling the matter.

The oracle was functioning from as early as the eleventh century B.C. By the sixth century B.C. it was wielding such power that no cult or institution was changed or introduced without cosulting the oracle first. Enquiries were also made concerning tactics in war and major political problems. Everything depended on the Pythia's inspired answers. Because of its extraordinary power and influence, opportunists were tempted to use the oracle for their own personal ambitions and political propaganda. On the whole, however, this seldom happened because the offender, if found out, was severely punished.

Interpreting some of the Pythia's answers often proved extremely perplexing. For example, when Athens was in danger from the Persians, the Pythia's advice to the envoys who had been sent from Athens to the oracle, had been to flee from the advancing enemy: *Miserable men, why are you sitting idle? Leave in flight the furthest dwellings of your land and the high peaks of the wheel-shaped town. For neither head nor body remains firm, nor tipmost toes nor hands; nor is anything of the middle left, but it is reduced to oblivion...*(Herodotus Bk7,140) The envoys had not dared return to Athens with this gloomy answer, so returned for a second enquiry. On that occasion Apollo responded with a grain of optimism: *...yet Zeus of the broad heaven gives to the Tritoborn a wooden wall, alone to remain undestroyed, and it will bless you and your children...* (Herodotus Book 7,141)

A wooden wall? The envoys bravely delivered this answer to the elders of Athens who puzzled over it. Some thought the wooden wall must be the palisade around the Acropolis, while others believed it was the Athenian ships which were made of timber. When the latter defeated the Persian fleet at Salamis, those who were of the opinion the 'wooden wall' was the Athenian fleet were proved correct.

There is also a legend that when the Persians attempted to invade Delphi, the gods caused thunder and lightning, and sent boulders tumbling from the pinnacle of the Phaedriades crags, crushing the invaders and putting them to flight.

Further on from the temple of Apollo is a small and damaged theatre of Dionysos, god of wine and drama. In its awesome setting performances must have been doubly dramatic. It is claimed that Apollo left his sanctuary for the three winter months of the year and, during his absence, it was Dionysos who presided there. In Apollo's absence there were no oracular enquiries.

On the highest terrace is a stadium where the foot-races of the Pythian Games were held. The remains of the entrance through which the athletes passed are still intact, as are the marble slabs set in the ground with holes in them for the posts which separated the athletes, and grooves in which to place their feet.

It is interesting how this famous pagan site survived into the Christian era. Constantine, the first Roman Emperor to accept Christianity as a true religion, took a number of the greatest works of art from Delphi to adorn his new city of Constantinople. It is known that Apollo's oracle was approached and questioned regarding Jesus, and had responded that Christ was a wise man who had worked miracles and had died a 'bitter death'. The miscreants, the oracle said, were the Christians who insisted on worshipping his mortal body when it had been torn and disfigured by nails. The Christian cult was absurd, and God incarnate a myth, the oracle concluded.

The last oracular pronouncement was deliverd to Julian the Apostate who had been brought up a Christian but wanted to return to paganism: *Tell the King, the fairwrought hall has fallen to the ground, no longer has Phoebos a hut, nor a prophetic laurel, nor a spring that speaks. The water of speech even is quenched.*

Not far from the museum at Delphi there is a well-preserved floor mosaic depicting geometric patterns and figures within medallions. This is from a fifth century church dedicated to St. George. Like Apollo who killed a python/dragoness, St. George killed a dragon. A few kilometres away from Delphi is the village of Aráchova where an annual three-day festival of St. George killing a local dragon is celebrated. The village has a church dedicated to St. George, and inside it is a column once part of a temple of Apollo.

The Christian version of the killing of a dragon at Aráchova is that there was once a monstrous dragon in the locality (Delphi?) who deprived the locals of their water. All attempts to persuade him to spare enough for the people failed until he set eyes on the king's daughter. Only if she was given to him, he said, would he leave the water for the people. The girl was on the point of being sacrificed, when St. George arrived and killed the dragon.

It was the Emperor Theodosius I, an ardent Christian, who finally closed down all the pagan sanctuaries and ended the oracle at Delphi. In time the whole site disappeared and the village of Kastri was built over it. In 1898, however, there was so much renewed interest in the ancient sanctuary, that the whole village was demolished, and the villagers rehoused in what is today's town of Delphi. Archaeologists then set to work and the present ruins of antiquity were again revealed. Today people come from all over the world to see this ancient site in its dramatic setting at the foot of Mt. Parnassos, and it is unlikely now that what remains of the Delphic oracle will ever be forgotten.

Denotes a separate booklet on the subject.

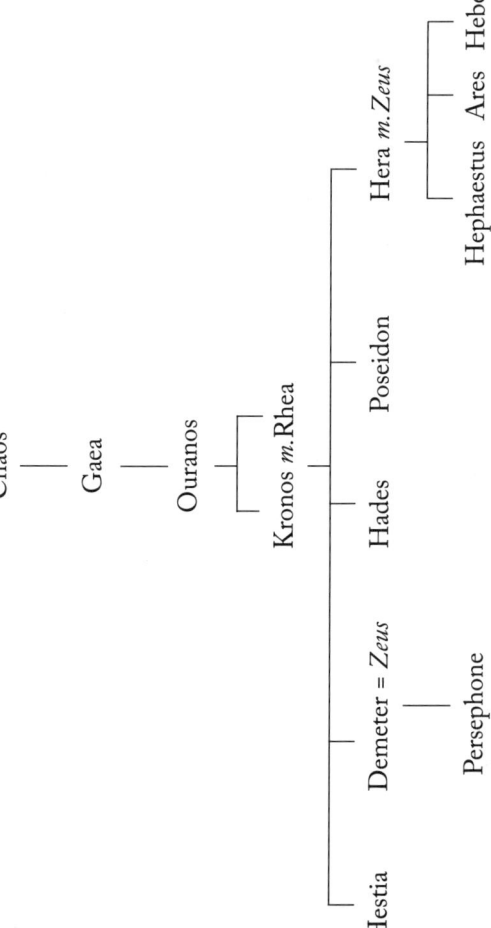

THE IMMORTAL GODS BORN OF ZEUS BY MORTAL WOMEN

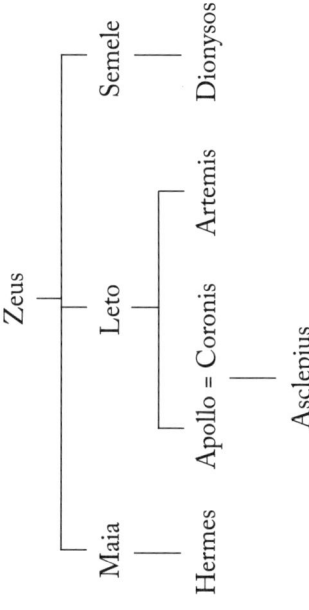

GLOSSARY OF GODS AND GODDESSES

APOLLO – Son of Zeus and the Titaness Leto. He was twin brother of Artemis, and god of medicine, music, archery and prophecy.

ARTEMIS – Daughter of Zeus and the Titaness Leto, and twin sister of Apollo. She was goddess of wild life, of hunting and also of very young things.

ATHENA – Daughter of Zeus and Metis (whose name means 'thought', 'counsel'). She was goddess of victory, weaving and handicraft, and also protectress of many cities, but especially Athens.

CHAOS – Primordial Chaos from which came Ouranos (the heavens) and Gaea (earth).

GAEA – The personification of the the earth, who sprang from Chaos.

HADES – Brother of Zeus and god of the underworld.

HERA – Wife and sister of Zeus. She was goddess of women and marriage.

KRONOS – A Titan, and married to Rhea who gave birth to many of the Olympian gods, including Hera and Zeus. His name means 'time'.

RHEA – A Titaness, and wife of Kronos. She was mother of Zeus and Hera.

TITANS – The offspring of Ouranos (often spelt Uranus, meaning the 'heavens') and Gaea (the earth). There were said to be twelve of them, six sons and six daughters. Kronos was one of the sons, and Rhea one of the daughters. These two gave birth to many of the Olympian gods.

ZEUS – Son of Kronos and Rhea. Supreme god of the ancient world. He was god of the heavens, giver of the laws, and dispenser of justice. It was often said that Apollo was his spokesman, and questions put to Apollo's oracle came from his father.

MORE FROM THE
PUT IT IN YOUR POCKET SERIES
GREEK MYTHS

TROJAN WAR
THE JUDGEMENT OF PARIS
HELEN
KING AGAMEMNON
ACHILLES
THE WOODEN HORSE
ODYSSEUS

ISLANDS
CHIOS – HOMER
CRETE – THESEUS AND THE MINOTAUR
KOS – HIPPOCRATES AND ASCLEPIUS
NAXOS – THESEUS AND ARIADNE
RHODES – THE COLOSSUS
SANTORINI – THE LOST ISLAND OF ATLANTIS

ALSO BY JILL DUDLEY

YE GODS! (TRAVELS IN GREECE)

YE GODS! II (MORE TRAVELS IN GREECE)

LAP OF THE GODS (TRAVELS IN CRETE
AND THE AEGEAN ISLANDS)